Studies in Musical Science & Philosophy
Vol 3

Abel's Temperament

Brian Capleton PhD

Adaptations from published papers

Dr Brian Capleton lectured in Piano Technology at the Royal National College, and is an alumnus of Wolfson College Oxford, the Royal College of Music, Trinity College of Music London, and Dartington College of Arts.

Published by Amarilli Books

Copyright © 2015, Brian Capleton

1st Edition

Content adapted from material submitted in
partial fulfilment of the requirements for the
Royal College of Music Master's degree.

ISBN 978-0-9928141-8-2

A CIP catalogue record for this book is available
from the British Library.

Thomas Gainsborough : Carl Friedrich Abel

Contents

Gainsborough's portrait of Abel

Gainsborough's portrait of Carl Friedrich Abel and his viol,[1] now in the National Portrait Gallery, is an arresting work both in its light and colour, and in its composition.

Unlike Gainsborough's portrait of Abel in the Huntington Library and Art Gallery,[2] the viol in the National Portrait Gallery painting is being held virtually in the playing position, offering considerable information about the instrument itself.

The belly and fingerboard almost face the observer, showing such features as a detailed rose, and unusual 'C holes'. Interestingly, the instrument has seven strings, although Abel's extant gamba compositions do not call for the low A string in the solo parts.

The portrait is thought to have been originally owned by one of Gainsborough's daughters, and was acquired by the Gallery in 1987. It was previously on public display at London's Grosvenor gallery in 1885, but for most of its provenance has been in private collections.[3]

In the painting, the brilliant golden yellow of the light on Abel's attire draws the eye, and in contrast, the dull brown colouring of the viol's frets - being almost identical to that of the fingerboard - cause this detail of the instrument to recede. Indeed, as the portrait was displayed in 1994, above eye level and with the canvass protected by glass, the 'higher' frets (further down the fingerboard towards the bridge) were barely visible.

Close scrutiny however, reveals significant detail in the frets, including a 'correct' graduation in their thicknesses from nut to bridge. On the 'lower', thicker frets (those nearer the nut), the double strand of gut is clearly depicted, showing the detail of the two strands separating slightly at the knot end, as one would expect to see on an actual instrument.

When viewed from a normal distance, there is one outstanding feature of the painting that any viol player will notice as strange. This is the 'unrealistic' spacing of the first three frets, and in particular the gap between the first and second frets.

Viol players will be familiar with the subject of viol frets and their positions on the instrument – it is not something that violists can ignore for long. The gut frets are tied around the neck of the viol – they are moveable, and replaceable. Indeed, they have to be replaced from time to time, as they are subject to wear, and eventually will break if left unattended.

The frets also have to be moved from their initial positions as the viol's strings age, because as the strings become older and more worn, there will be changes to the precise pitches of the notes they produce at given stopping positions. Experienced players will also move the frets for many other reasons, including the accommodation of a tuning or temperament on other instruments, with which the viol is being played.

For most viol players with some experience, the fret positioning is never merely an accepted feature of the instrument. On the contrary, the fret positions are usually a matter of conscious choice, depending on the tuning results for which the player is aiming, and the condition of the instrument and its strings.

Could we regard Gainsborough's painting as providing 'iconographical evidence' for Abel's fret positions in practice? If so, then we might also have evidence for an unusual tuning system that Abel used, or perhaps preferred. We might naturally expect an artist of Gainsborough's calibre to reliably depict detail, but as it happens, in this particular case our expectations would be heightened more by what we know about Gainsborough, Abel and the viol.

Gainsborough was a very close friend and pupil of Abel, and after arriving in Bath in 1759, moved in musical circles that included the violinist Giardini, the Linley family and Johann Christian Fischer.[4] Contemporary reports placed him in the context of a professional musical environment [5] (where inevitably, he was sometimes the subject of good-natured 'fun-poking' by his professional colleagues).[6]

According to Angelo he had 'tried his native skill upon almost every instrument', and was passionately devoted to music to such an extent that Angelo thought 'there were times when music appeared his employment, and painting his diversion'.[7] Gainsborough was an accomplished violinist,[8] but it was in fact the viol that was his most loved instrument.

The Reverend Henry Bate, himself an accomplished 'cellist,[9] described Gainsborough's sensibilities as a viol player as 'very near indeed to Abel's standard'.[10] We would indeed expect Gainsborough to have been very acquainted with the details of the viol's setup. Gainsborough himself owned five viols,[11] and his interest in the form and construction of musical instruments generally, was noted by William Jackson, who reported the pleasure

Gainsborough took in observing a violin 'for many minutes, in silence'.[12]

So what does Gainsborough's portrait of Abel and his viol tell us, in this respect? As is often the case in examining 'evidence', the process of looking for 'answers' produces more questions. The actual measurements for the fret positions[13] are as follows (the measurements were taken along the surface of the glass covering the canvass, so any normal expected error is likely to have increased by error due to parallax):

Nut-fret distance (cm)				Bridge-fret distance (cm)			
Fret number	C string	D1 string	D6 string	Fret number	C string	D1 string	D6 string
1	4	3.9	3.7	1	69.4	69	68.6
2	8.6	8.5	8.5	2	64.7	64.4	64
3	12.2	12.2	12	3	61	60.6	60.4
4	15.7	15.6	15.5	4	57.7	57.2	57
5	18.4	18.4	18.3	5	54.7	54.3	54.2
6	21	21.1	20.8	6	52.1	51.6	51.6
7	23.6	23.7	23.3	7	49.4	49	49

From these measurements alone it is clear that the viol in the painting is probably very close to 'life size'. A maximum string length of around 73 or 74 cm is about what we might expect for a large, seven string viol. Once in possession of measurements, it is easy to empirically recreate the fret positioning on a viol of the same string length, or proportional positioning on a viol of similar string length.

If we do this, the empirical result is interesting, not because it provides an immediate insight into certain tuning preferences, but precisely because it appears to be entirely impractical. The frets turn out to be literally nowhere near positions that would allow a 'normal' workable tuning of the instrument, even taking into account the variations that might occur due to ageing strings of different kinds and/or different conditions.

They are not even where one might expect to find them if they had 'migrated' from their proper positions, perhaps on an instrument that it not very much used now. Would Gainsborough have ignored this detail of an instrument, or exercised 'artistic license' to such a degree on this one aspect of the portrait?

The portrait was apparently in poor condition when it arrived at the National Portrait Gallery, and was subject to restoration work. Could the restoration have provided the painting with spurious fret positions? Surely we should not assume this kind of error, without further evidence. So what interpretation can we make?

The frets could have been added to the instrument just for the purposes of the portrait, without the instrument having been played first, or Gainsborough could simply have attached no importance to the accurate depiction of fret positions.

The latter is probably also unlikely. It is perhaps more sensible to argue that the fret positions are depicted according Gainsborough's sense of 'visual proportion' appropriate to the composition of the painting, thus representing real fret positions in a visually, but not quantitatively correct way. If this is the case, then there is still some interesting information to be gleaned from their depicted positioning.

Even had there been unquestionable fret positions in the portrait, we would not expect to demonstrate this or that specific temperament to have been definitely in use, but rather, a more general 'class' or 'type'. To see the reason for this, before we make an interpretation, and to see how the land lies with respect to viols and temperaments generally, we should first take a detour into the subject of temperament.

Temperament

The concept of musical temperament is mentioned as early as 1496 in Gafurio's *Practica musicae*,[14] in which he refers to an already existing practice of tempering rather than a new idea. The general concern with the relationship of musical intervals and arithmetic ratios has far older documented origins.

Even the well known, explicit (but enigmatic) references to these relationships that appear in Plato's *Timeaus*, reiterate an existing lineage of ideas to which allusions also appear in pre-Socratic sources, and whose origin is attributed to Pythagoras (fl. BC 530).[15] The basic tenets of temperament theory then, concerning the way 'untempered' musical intervals are represented mathematically, are not disconnected from the 'Pythagorean tradition' in general.

The 'traditional' mathematical expression of temperament theory is (like many scientific theories) an idealised, approximate theory – it is a further development from the ancient (and by ascription, Pythagorean) science of 'harmonics'.

It is built on certain ratios assumed to 'define' musical intervals arithmetically, that we now know can indeed be justified as approximately true, on the basis of the acoustical structure of some musical tones, especially those from strings and pipes. Hitherto, the 'inventors' of temperaments did not have the knowledge of the complex acoustical structure of musical tones in mathematical terms, that we have today.

What was originally known, and attributed to Pythagoras, was the reliably accurate (but not mathematically perfect) relationship between tensioned string lengths and musical 'pitch', a relationship approximately reiterated by organ pipes. This relationship does yield simple, whole number ratios, like 3:2 for a perfect fifths and 2:1 for an octave.

The 'history of science' would tend to consider Pythagoras for his 'contributions to science', regarding him in the role of an 'early scientist'. But a notably different Pythagoras is seen by other disciplines, and by a considerable body of sources from before the so-called 'scientific revolution', and also by the many later sources that were still part of the 'intellectual culture' of deference to the ancients.

What we see here, is Pythagoras the Divine, the mystic, the numerologist, the healer, and the 'hearer' of the 'harmony of the spheres'. It is not actually from a sheer confidence in the discovered laws of natural phenomena, that the simple arithmetic ratios, and even the mathematics of temperament theory, acquired their original 'authority'. Rather, this was inherited from their relationship with the venerable 'Pythagorean tradition' that gave the original endorsement to the ratios for the perfect intervals.

This 'tradition' has not been without its opponents,[16] but nonetheless has enjoyed considerable influence as being based on the 'authority' of ancient wisdom. We find this influence repeatedly appearing, whether overtly or covertly, in many important sources including, for example, Boethius and Ptolemy.

Boethius will already be familiar to musicologists. Claudius Ptolemy (c. AD 75), who may be less familiar to musicians and musicologists, was responsible for the model of the 'Ptolemaic universe' or celestial system,[17] with the Earth at the centre, that predominated for fifteen centuries until the so-called 'scientific revolution' of the seventeenth century.

At the beginning of his extensive three-book treatise entitled *Harmonics*, he states that the student of *harmonics* must aim 'to preserve the hypotheses of the *kanon*' (a stringed instrument), and that the astronomer must aim 'to preserve the hypotheses concerning the movements of the heavenly bodies...'.[18]

These 'hypotheses' derive from the divinely ordained connection between certain whole number ratios, musical intervals, the motions of the planets, and the human soul.[19] The Church's endorsement of geocentricity may have been connected with 'metaphysical' dogma, but the relevant sections of Ptolemy's *Harmonics* are mathematically intense – so much so that he has been quite justly described as a 'number cruncher'.[20]

Because it was based on 'ancient authority' transmitted by Plato, and according to the attestations, derived from Pythagoras, the quantitative part of Ptolemy's work was very influential, very complex, – and whilst mathematically correct, very mistaken.

In a sense, temperament theory has in the past enjoyed the same umbrella of authority, even though in its own right, its 'fit' to the acoustics of musical instruments is arguably better than the 'fit' of Ptolemaic astronomy to actual planetary motions.

Today, temperament theory remains a very useful way of sensibly modelling acoustical tuning results on musical instruments – best of all pipe organs and stringed keyboard instruments.[21] But in itself it is essentially an arithmetic theory of number relationships, really applicable only to instruments whose tones have acoustical structures that are reasonably close to harmonic.[22]

It is, or should be, regarded like many other scientific theories - as a convenient approximation, and not as a divinely ordained absolute. The musical perfect fifth is not in itself a string length ratio. It is an acoustical consonance. The consonance occurs because of the acoustical structure of the tones, whether in strings, pipes, or the human voice.

On strings, it is this that causes the Pythagorean string length ratios to exist, not *vice versa*. When, for example, we apply harmonic temperament theory to the metallophones of the Gamelan, bells, gongs, or tuned drums, it becomes relatively vague, inappropriate, or even meaningless.

Even applied to organs and harpsichords it should always be remembered that it is not an 'absolute' model or a true physical theory for the acoustics of these instruments, despite its precision in dealing with say, '1/4 comma' as distinct from '1/5 comma' or '2/7 comma'.

Most temperaments, however vaguely described when they were first documented, are now 'translated' into a mathematically defined form. Without the pre-defined association of ratios such as 3:2 for a perfect fifth, or 2:1 for an octave, temperament theory as we know it and use it today, ceases to exist.

Being based on the pure mathematical relationships of numbers, and in the first instance on simple, whole number ratios, the construction of different temperaments as various twelve note divisions of the octave, is very much a matter of mathematical precision.[23]

In acoustical terms, the practical need for tempering arises from the fact that very small, microtonal intervals (for example the *commas*, *dieses* or *schisma*), appear between the different results of tuning a given set of notes through different tuning sequences.

These microtonal intervals are themselves divided and distributed in various ways through the musical intervals that occur in the chromatic scale, according to the specific temperament in use. They include, for example, the syntonic comma whose typically small (close to unity) associated ratio is 81:80.

This microtonal interval is then divided in various temperaments into even smaller intervals, up to around a twelfth of the size, and sometimes even smaller. What mathematically defines one temperament as distinct from another then, is a distribution of ratios defined to this order of accuracy.

When we distinguish between say, quarter-comma meantone and fifth comma meantone, we are talking about differences between the two scales ranging from about a twelfth of a semitone to less than a ninetieth of a semitone.[24] Only if when in use, an instrument's tuning stability remains well inside these limits, can we truly of speak of such clearly defined different temperaments as existing on the instrument in question.

Tuning in practice

As far as practical tuning is concerned there are three things to consider. The first is how well the 'whole number ratio' premisses of temperament theory 'fit' the actual acoustical nature of the musical instrument to which we are attempting to apply it.

The second - if such a good 'fit' exists - is what means are employed to ensure that the tuning result in practice, represents with fidelity the theoretical prescription. The third, is whether this precision of tuning actually remains in place whilst the instrument is in use.

The idea of this or that temperament being present on an instrument, as defined by temperament theory, is therefore only meaningful to the degree to which (a) the acoustics of the instrument comply with the premisses of temperament theory, *and* (b), a properly accurate means of applying the temperament is employed, *and* (c), the tuning stability of the instrument in use, matches the precision with which the temperament is defined.

In the case of an organ or harpsichord, we could argue the use of an electronic meter would provide an accurate means of tuning. (However, we should certainly not trust the popular notion that a single meter dial, being electronic, must therefore provide the 'last word' in accuracy).[25]

Fortunately, harpsichord strings do generally conform closely to the expectations of temperament theory, provided the instrument's tuning stability is satisfactory. Viols on the other hand, behave quite differently.

Compared to the tuning of temperaments on the harpsichord, significant changes to the note produced by the viol string arise not only from turning the peg (the equivalent of turning the wrest pin on a harpsichord), but also from the pressure of the bowing, and the pressure applied by the finger for a stopped noted. The note also varies with the exact finger stopping position.

Variations caused by any of these factors can cause changes that in play, can violate the level of precision necessary for a genuine temperament definition, as accurately applied to the keyboard. In addition to the notes having tuning characteristics that are unstable or not fixed, viol strings themselves present further difficulties.

A characteristic known in musical acoustics as *inharmonicity*, which causes the actual physical behaviour of strings to 'disagree' with the premises of temperament theory, is inevitably present to a relatively high degree in the relatively short, low tension, gut based viol strings. Wear and ageing of the strings can make the effect of *inharmonicity* very large indeed.[26]

The effect of this alone, and not least the fact that it will be present in markedly different degrees in the different strings across the viol, including strings of different ages, construction and condition, compromises the 'fit' between the acoustics of the strings and the expectations of temperament theory.

One of the least recognised features of viol tone, but one disruptive to temperament definition, is *falseness*. Many viol players will have been frustrated by occasional acute string *falseness* at some time, when attempting to tune the viol, perhaps assuming this characteristic of string behaviour to be some kind of 'wolf' in the instrument.

In musician's terminology, a *false* string has more than one pitch. Its pitch will typically cycle between a maximum and a minimum if it is plucked. The difference between the two pitches can in a bad case be in the order of a whole comma (about a quarter of a semitone) or more, when the string is plucked.

It would not be an exaggeration to say that most viols strings are false, to some degree – but if the rate of alternation is slow enough compared with the decay rate, or the pitch variation is small enough, it will not be noticed. Bowing can steady the tone, but the same level of imprecision can remain in the effect of bowing.

Thus we may tune and fret a viol according to a temperament prescription for a keyboard, or a mathematical definition, but in the event of playing we will not genuinely be playing in that temperament as mathematically defined. Furthermore the acoustical characteristics of our scale and intervals as played on the viol, will not be precisely the same as those on the harpsichord tuned to the same temperament.

The original 'idea' or 'purpose' of the temperament as devised the keyboard, in terms of interval qualities, may be sometimes compromised, and other times even lost on the viol. Remarkably, this will be the case even if we tune and match note for note unisons with the harpsichord.[27]

What all this means is that we cannot measure precise fret positions to several decimal places and expect to 'reverse engineer' this data to indicate a precise temperament 'designed' for a keyboard, and defined in terms of a precise division of a comma.

Nevertheless, there are meaningful, general statements we *can* make about viol temperament, provided we understand that there is a difference between the meanings of 'temperament' applied to a viol, a harpsichord, or a mathematical description.

Even with the vaguest data we might be able to do this, for the simple reason that all temperaments can be classified in broad generic classes, and some classes produce recognisable patterns in fret spacing. Thus, we can distinguish between say, fretting that looks like 'a meantone', or fretting that looks like 'an extreme meantone'. We can also recognise an 'equal temperament' fretting, roughly speaking.

From the point of view of historical musicology, one would expect to try to match the temperament with one of those that documented evidence suggests existed, or were in use at the time, and possibly in the same region or place.

On an instrument such as the viol, this does not, however, preclude the existence of 'temperaments' that are apparently anachronistic from the point of view of other such evidence.

Given the imprecision of temperament definition applied to the viol, anything is possible. Thus what qualifies on the viol as 'equal temperament', appears on viols in the sixteenth century, when the methods for its precision application to keyboards did not become generally available until the nineteenth century.

The reason is that a rough 'pseudo equal temperament' that does not meet the precision and characteristics we would expect of it today, is relatively easy to produce or 'stumble on' empirically. The same is true of many other temperaments, because a 'temperament' arrangement of some kind must naturally occur in a scale not tuned to the Pythagorean ideal, whether by design or accident.

We *could* argue that a particular so-called 'temperament' on the viol, could not have existed at a given time, because it was not 'discovered', 'invented' or documented until later. But in practice this is rather like stating rusty iron could not have existed before the documentation of the process of oxidisation, or the discovery of oxygen.

Thus, in the case of the viol, data analysis is a sensible way to proceed in the first instance. We cannot really work with precise data to produce precise conclusions, but we can use precise data to produce general conclusions, which as we shall see, is in this case probably best expressed simply through the visual matching of fret space patterns.

Temperament classes

'Traditionally', temperaments are often mathematically defined in theory using the Pythagorean Circle or Great Circle of fifths:

Fig 1:

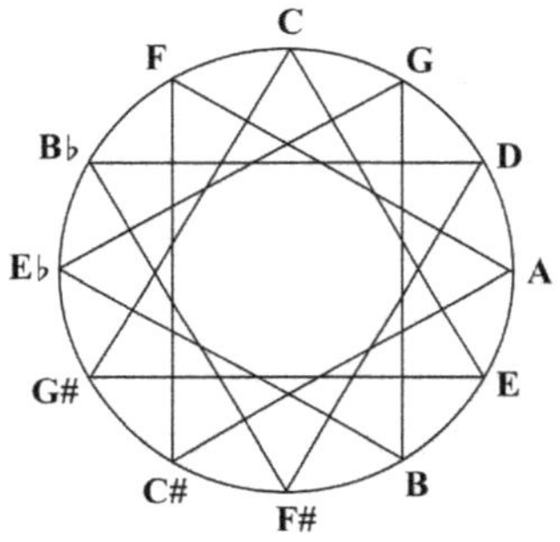

In this particular example (Fig 1), rising fifths appear clockwise round the circle as far as G sharp, and falling fifths appear anticlockwise to E flat. Nominally, the interval G sharp rising to E flat, is a diminished minor sixth, not a fifth.

The practical counterpart to this model is that starting on C, we could tune a whole chromatic scale by tuning first the clockwise sequence of notes C, G, D, A, etc. as far as G sharp, and then the anticlockwise sequence. In practice we can 'invert' any rising fifth and tune a falling fourth instead.

Similarly we can invert any falling fifth and tune a rising fourth instead. For example, a practical sequence using perfect fifths or their inversions to construct a chromatic scale within one octave of the compass might be:

Fig 2

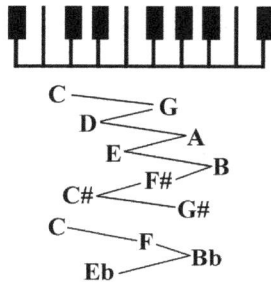

If we complete the scale by tuning the C an octave above the starting C, as a 'perfect' octave, we would then find that the rising fourth and fifth formed from G and F in the scale to the upper C, would turn out to be perfect too.

However, the untuned interval formed between G sharp and E flat - the notes at the ends of the sequences - will not be a perfect fifth. Nor will it sound like one. It will be the infamous 'wolf' interval that is musically unusable – a 'fifth' that is far too small or 'narrow'. The amount by which this 'wolf' deviates from a perfect fifth is the Pythagorean comma, about 24 cents or a quarter of a semitone.[28]

A comma is only a microtonal interval, but a fifth only needs to be 'mistuned' by a microtonal interval in order to become too grossly mistuned to be musically acceptable. In short, twelve perfect fifths will not 'fit into' an octave, whichever sequence of fifths and inversions we choose.

The root *physical* cause of this lies in the 'internal' acoustical structure of the musical tone produced by things

25

like strings and pipes. Pythagoras, whose name the comma bears, did not know this, but apparently did know about the relationship of tensioned string lengths and musical pitch, which in fact has its roots in the same cause. The mathematical part of the model consists of representing the musical intervals, and all the relationships between them, as ratios round the Circle.[29]

In Fig 1 or Fig 2 the ratio for any interval can be derived from the product of the ratios of all the intervals sequenced to make it. As long as we obey the necessary rules for manipulating the arithmetic, we will get the same results whether we use sequences round the Pythagorean Circle or a sequence like that in Fig 2. The Circle is probably the more useful way of displaying sequences, for deriving the ratios for intervals other than fifths.

The straight lines in Fig 1, for example, connect notes that clockwise form rising major thirds, unless the arc of the Circle containing the sequence includes the 'wolf' G sharp to E flat. In this case the interval is of course nominally a diminished fourth.

The four fifths round the arc across the straight line 'define' the size of the third. If the four fifths are genuine 'perfect' fifths (each with a mathematical ratio 3:2), the third will be excessively large (a 'Pythagorean third' with a ratio 81:64, rather than 5:4, the harmonic ratio for a 'pure' third).

By *tempering* some or all of the fifths narrow, (i.e. in effect 'mistuning' them slightly), the size of third can be controlled. Also, by reducing the size of the eleven tempered fifths in the sequence, the size of the last remaining interval can be improved, and made musically usable.

We could of course draw straight lines connecting notes that 'define' semitones, rather than major thirds, Fig 3:

Fig 3

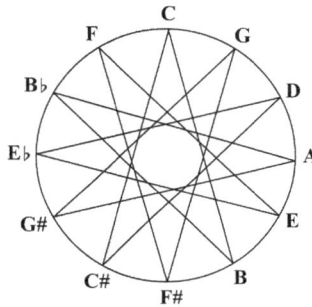

Clearly then, the size of any semitone will also be 'defined' by the chosen sizes of the tempered fifths (or 'non fifths') in the sequence or arc of the Circle across its straight line.

Temperaments do not necessarily consist of a set of eleven deliberately tuned or tempered fifths, always leaving the last 'fifth' or wolf interval untuned.

Many temperaments employ the deliberate tuning or tempering of all twelve fifths. The former kind, require tuning or tempering two sequences round the Circle, first one way, and then the other, leaving one interval untuned. These are thus called *non circulating* temperaments. The latter kind could be tuned in a continuous sequence right round the Circle. These are *circulating* temperaments.

If all the tuned fifths are tempered by the same amount, the temperament is said to be a *regular temperament*. If they are tempered by different amounts, the temperament is said to be *irregular*.

All non circulating, regular temperaments that temper eleven of the twelve intervals round the Circle, are now referred to in contemporary theory as 'meantone' temperaments, because the size of the tone is half the size of the major third, across arcs that do not include the 'wolf' interval.

This set of all such temperaments is complemented with the addition of Equal Temperament, in which *all* the fifths round the Circle are tempered by the same amount. Equal Temperament is the only *circulating* meantone temperament.[30]

Pietro Aron appears to be have been the first to document a meantone temperament in 1523,[31] without any mathematical description, and what he described is now recognised mathematically as '1/4 comma meantone'. In this temperament eleven fifths are tempered narrow by ¼ syntonic comma (about 1/20 semitone), a reasonable maximum amount of tempering one would expect to find in fifths.

Despite the fact that history shows a process of 'inventing' or 'discovering' numerous temperaments, sometimes empirically, sometimes mathematically, all the possibilities for temperaments of any kind, derived from the 'Pythagorean' or harmonic ratios, can be encapsulated in, and predicted from *generalised* laws.[32]

Any temperament, whether circulating or non circulating, can in fact be simply written as an array of twelve quantities, including the 'wolf', if necessary. Today we have computer power to do any tedious mathematical 'donkey work' for us, so it is actually just as easy to express any temperament as a mathematical vector, and to manipulate data in matrices if necessary.

The fret positions in Gainsborough's painting, was first analysed by the author in 1994 using computer spreadsheet analysis,[33] but the following results were obtained by direct graphing from vector formulae.[34]

Abel's frets

We can represent the fingerboard horizontally, for convenience, with the nut on the left and the bridge off towards the right. The strings in this case would be, from top to bottom, D(1st), A(2nd), E(3rd), C(4th), G(5th), D(6th), A(7th). The height of the frets in the diagrams is arbitrary, and we will number the frets 1 to 7 from left to right.

Abel's frets in the painting can then be represented as follows, with the positioning of frets for Equal Temperament on the same strings, compared above:

Fig 4

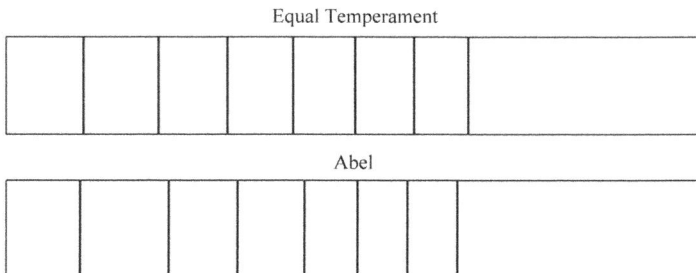

Equal Temperament

Abel

It is convenient to speak of musical interval sizes in cents (hundredths of a semitone). We can then also speak of fret positions and spacings in cents. Thus to say fret 1 is 100 cents from the nut would mean the fret is positioned so that the note stopped on it is 100 cents above the open string note.

We are, of course, now deliberately neglecting variations that would be due finger stopping positions, bowing pressures, and other problems. Equal Temperament provides a good starting point for comparison.

Taken literally, the fret positions do not correspond visually to any recognisable positioning that one would expect to find if the viol was tuned to any practical temperament. The second, third and fourth frets are all impracticably 'high' (near the bridge), and the sixth and seventh frets are impracticably 'low' (near the nut).

The first and fifth frets are about right. It seems unlikely that the seventh fret would be positioned unfavourably with respect to the note it stops on the first string, so the interval from the open first string (D) to its seventh fret stopped note (A) would reasonably be expected to form a musically usable interval.

The diagrams give some immediate idea of the situation, but the severity is not immediately obvious. For a better appreciation, consider the following: The diagram shows the seventh fret is quite 'flat' compared to its Equal Temperament position.

Theoretically, if the seventh fret were tuned 1/4 comma flat (1/4 comma being a reasonable maximum tempering to expect in the interval D-A), it would be positioned 696 cents from the nut. It is in fact positioned 17 cents (about 1/6 semitone) flat of the 'quarter comma' position, which makes the interval with the open string definitely a 'wolf'.

Inharmonicity due to string age and wear may cause frets to be moved back towards the nut in some instances, but by this distance would be most unusual, and this does not account for the very 'sharp' positions of the second, third, and fourth frets.

Viol players will easily grasp the impracticality of the fret positioning from the following: If the open first string (D), were tuned to make an octave with the D stopped on the second fret of the fourth (C) string, then the open second string (A), would have to be tuned 36 cents (more than a third of a semitone) flatter than a pure fourth below the first (D) string, in order for the C stopped on its third fret to make an octave with the open C string.

There is one way that we could explain the overall positioning of the sixth and seventh frets. If the action was very high, the distance from the strings to the fingerboard in this region would be great.

Stopping the strings on such a viol in these high positions, considerably increases the string tension, so the frets are correspondingly moved back towards the nut. What this still does not explain, is the positioning of the first three or four frets, and the unrealistically large space between the first and second frets, which are so immediately noticeable on the painting.

Scaled positioning

Assuming Gainsborough used a sense of 'artistic visual proportion', rather than taking measurements, we can make adjustments to take into account Abel's seventh fret position as depicted by the painting, so that our representation of Equal Temperament, given a suitable scale mapping from the data, agrees with the painting on the position of the seventh fret.

By doing this, we can see if the painted frets appear to be a good 'artistic visual proportion' representation of an Equal Temperament spacing. The results are then:

Fig 5

Equal Temperament

Abel

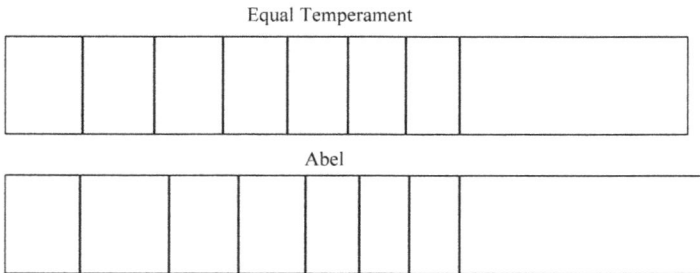

The results are not a very convincing portrayal of Equal Temperament spacing. Similarly, just for demonstration purposes, we can carry out the same procedure for meantone varieties:

Fig 6

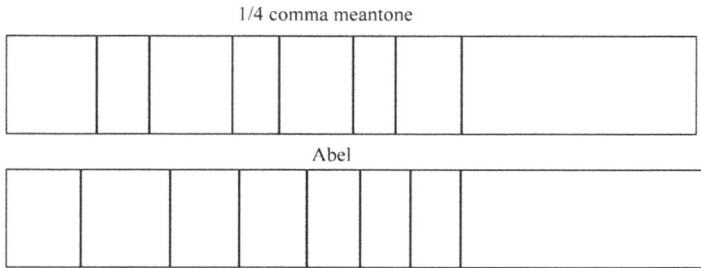

1/4 comma meantone

Abel

Fig 6 shows one natural extreme, the quarter comma meantone (with the wolf nominally G sharp to E flat). Here, the first fret is positioned for a B flat on the A string rather than a C sharp on the C string, which is an option that might typically be chosen if one had to tune the viol to meantone.

One characteristic effect of the wolf in the meantone Circle, is that any intervals between notes joined by an arc that includes the wolf, will be a different size to the same intervals between notes joined across other arcs of the Circle.

The consequence of this that there are two sizes of semitone in meantone temperament, which are clearly visible in the diagram. Fig 7 shows the same for the less extreme example of 1/8 comma meantone.

Fig 7

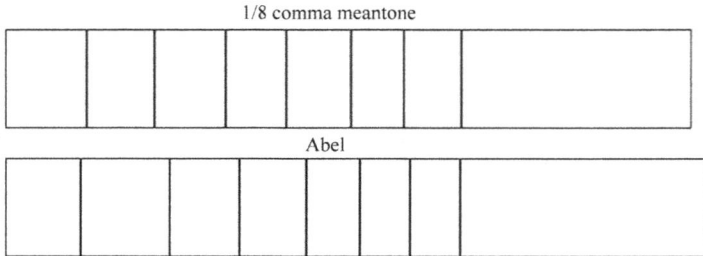

1/8 comma meantone

Abel

In Equal Temperament all intervals of any one kind are the same size, resulting in spaces between the frets that diminish exponentially. The resultant visual pattern of smoothly decreasing spaces can be seen from Fig 4 or Fig 5. It is clear even visually, from the Abel frets, that we would be dealing with an unequal temperament, and from the above, not a meantone.

Any temperament other than Equal Temperament will demand that some frets (notably the first and sixth) need to be in different positions for different strings. One practical answer to this is to position the fret correctly for one or more strings, at the expense of the others. We did this with the first fret in the meantone diagrams.

Splitting the two strands of fret-gut apart to provide more than one position is another possibility, but the painting definitely shows no signs of this. It is of course also possible to place the fret at a compromise position between the 'correct' positions for different strings.

These factors make the painted frets particularly difficult to interpret. In practice, frets may also be moved from recognisable positions based on a recognisable temperament, purely to accommodate specific intervals in a particular piece of music. This is done to improve sonority, and to overcome stopped note pitch anomalies caused by inharmonicity in the string behaviour.

It is possible for a string to 'stop flat' on certain frets, requiring the fret to be moved towards the bridge, but it is more common for it to 'stop sharp', in which case the fret is moved back towards the nut. In the scaled depiction where the seventh fret is assumed to be in a 'sensible' position, the most striking feature of the Abel frets is that all the frets except the first and seventh, are positioned very 'high', i.e. shifted towards the bridge.

Another way of 'normalising', ignoring the seventh fret position, is to make the second fret positions agree for both Abel and Equal Temperament mapped for the same strings. Why the second fret? On the seventh fret none of the stopped notes are 'accidentals' for which there may be enharmonic variations for its position in an unequal temperament.

The second fret is similarly a good choice because there is only one accidental, the F sharp on the E string, but there are other good reasons. The open strings effectively make the viol an 'instrument in D'. It would be arguably very unlikely to favour a tuning without good octaves between the open D strings and the stopped D on the second fret of the C string.

Similar arguments apply also to the two open A strings on the seven string instrument, and the stopped A on the second fret of the G string. If we scale to align the second fret of a sequence for Equal temperament with the second of the painted frets on Abel's viol, we get the following visual result:

Fig 8

Equal Temperament

Abel

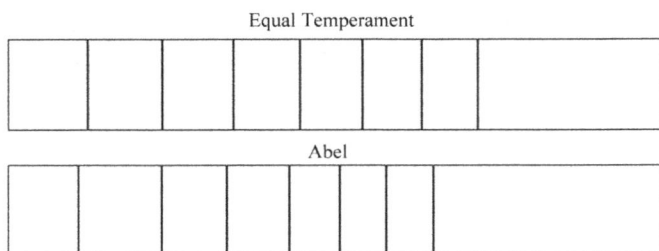

Now we can see that except for the first fret, the Abel frets could arguably be a depiction of Equal Temperament, but with the 'artistic license' allowing the exponential diminution of fret spacing towards the bridge, to be shown rather overzealously. What of that first fret?

One answer may immediately suggest itself to viol players themselves. It is not unusual for the first fret to be moved back towards the nut, for several reasons, on a viol otherwise basically tuned in Equal Temperament. This may be to provide a 'sweeter' (less tempered wide, or more 'pure') third between F sharp/G flat on the second fret of the E string, and A sharp/B flat on the first fret of the A string.

It also often provides a better F on the first fret of the E string, where this note stops sharp (as it frequently does, on the thicker E string). A flattened F is usually desirable to improve the fourth from the open C string to the F, which because it involves one open and one stopped string, can be particularly sonorous.

Lastly, it may also assist the tuning of the F major chord from the F on the bottom D string. This interpretation in no way conclusive, but might constitute a reasonable guess to explain what is otherwise a puzzling lack of accuracy in the painting.

The outstanding problem that this argument does not resolve, is that even considering moving the first fret back, the gap between the first and second frets is still visually, simply too large to be convincing. As we have said, this is the most immediately disquieting feature of the fret spacing, when one sees the painting itself.

The tonality of Abel's viol compositions

Can we glean any clues from the tonalities that Abel uses in his compositions? Abel's compositions, as might perhaps be expected, do not exploit remote tonalities. His symphonic writing never explores keys requiring more than four sharps or flats, and three flats are more common than three sharps.[35]

The viol works are even more restricted. The manuscript in New York,[36] containing virtuoso solo works, contains 23 pieces in D major, 2 in A major and 4 in D minor. These pieces appear to be music that Abel himself might have played.

The somewhat larger collection of duos and solos in the Countess of Pembroke's music book,[37] in the British

Library, exhibits a somewhat more puzzling restriction of tonalities. It explores only the major keys C, G, D, A, E, and modulates as far as the tonality of B major.

The B flat is used only rarely, and further flats do not occur. Changes of harmony from C major to F major or modulations to D minor, happen infrequently, and never so as to establish a full modulation bearing a repeated or new theme.

One could argue these restrictions were to suit the technique of the pupil for whom the pieces were written. Elizabeth Pembroke (1738 – 30th April 1831), wife of the 10th Earl Pembroke, was not a professional musician.

None of the thirty-six compositions are truly virtuoso pieces, and the bass parts may be very suitable for beginners, but many pieces in the solo part, although not unduly difficult, would require more than merely a beginner's competence.

The autograph, unaccompanied Sonata in G, is endorsed 'composed for the Lady Pembroke' and would require a fair level of competence in an amateur player – certainly a competence that should not, for example, exclude playing pieces in D minor or A minor.

If Elizabeth Pembroke was playing this Sonata, then it is reasonable to presume she was playing the solo parts in the accompanied pieces, rather than the easy bass, which weakens the supposition that the restrictions were to accommodate her lack of technique.

It is true that the avoidance, on the viol, of keys with more than four sharps in the key signature, would come as no surprise. Also, for inexperienced hands B flat major and E flat major on the viol can be awkward. But the total avoidance of A minor, G minor, and almost complete avoidance of D minor and F major, in a collection of thirty-six pieces written for the Countess,[38] does seem strange.

The key restrictions are consistent with those that would be expected had a meantone temperament been in use, and would also be consistent with the use of an unequal temperament that in the usual way favoured the quality of the major thirds in the 'home' keys. However, these kinds of temperament would not normally prevent the use of the keys that remain unexploited in the manuscript.

The natural resonance characteristics of the viol would explain the avoidance of the flat keys which can be very dull on the viol, but this does not apply to D minor, not least because the viol has two open D strings and at least one open A string. The consideration of resonance fails also to explain the avoidance of A minor and to a lesser extent G minor.

My own impression is that the key restrictions are probably not connected with temperament choice, and only partly, if at all, with resonance or technique considerations. The key restrictions seem likely to remain an unanswered question.

Lbl Add. 34007

Some more insight might be gained from a manuscript fragment in the British Library, inscribed *The Pure Method of Tuning the Harpsichord, According to Abel*, in Lbl Add. 34007. This manuscript consists mostly of compositions, but also contains the fragment purporting to be Abel's method of harpsichord tuning.

Of the baroque composers, it is probably JS Bach whom musicians and musicologists would first think of in relation to harpsichord tuning. The notion of JS Bach as an adept of tuning 'well tempered' harpsichords is as familiar as the title *Das Wohltemperierte Klavier*, of the forty eight preludes and fugues.

However, it is of course not just Bach who would have needed to be skilled at harpsichord tuning, but harpsichordists in general, including Abel, who was himself listed in Mortimer's *London Universal Directory*, 1763, as a harpsichord teacher.[39]

Harpsichordists have a choice of temperaments to which the harpsichord can be tuned, and we would expect competent harpsichordists to have a knowledge of tempering principles, and perhaps temperament theory.

We would expect, as we find today, that certain temperaments would be preferred. Where viols are played with a harpsichord, then the viol tuner is often subservient to the harpsichordist's tuning – the harpsichord will be tuned as desired, and the viol must accommodate. But the reverse could be true, especially if the harpsichord tuner or ensemble director is a violist, as would have been the case with Abel.

However, whatever the apparent choices of temperament, the 'note for note' matching of a harpsichord tuning with a viol's notes - both the open strings and the stopped notes - is not actually possible, in theory, except in the case where both instruments are tuned to Equal Temperament. Equal Temperament, in which all semitones are acoustically the same 'size', might therefore seem to be the natural choice for a violist who has to play together with a harpsichord.

The problem is, that equal tempering gives both the harpsichordist and the violist equally tempered major thirds, which are considerably wide (2/3 comma) and which many harpsichordists and violists find objectionable, at least in the 'home' keys.

The instructions given in the manuscript are reproduced in Fig 9:

Fig 9

Where this mark | is, bear a little upward

The first sequence, to bar **24**, is circulating, and the second sequence, from bars **25** to **44** is non-circulating, the break in the sequence being after bar **38**, and the position of any potential 'wolf' fifth being in the conventional position of G sharp to E flat. Both sequences are irregular, so we would not expect any interpretation to look like Equal Temperament in fret spacing, but it might look something like a meantone.

Since there are no other tempering instructions, it is reasonable to suppose that the instruction to 'bear up a little' at the vertical line mark, signifies points of deviation from an otherwise regular temperament. The unmarked fifths would have to be tempered narrow, otherwise the result of both sequences taken literally, would consist of a temperament comprising 8 untempered 'pure' fifths, 2 fifths tempered *wide*, and a 'wolf'.

Deliberately tempering fifths *wide* exacerbates the very need of temperament, and seems illogical, however, such a thing is not unheard of - schemes including wide tempered fifths do exist, for example, the Temperament ordinaire.

Instructions for harpsichord tuning in late eighteenth century England indicating simply that all the fifths should be tuned a little narrow, without being more specific than this, were not unusual.

This could constitute a kind of rough 'pseudo equal temperament'[40] that could be 'tweaked' to favour certain tonalities if desired. Or if the phrase 'all the fifths' is not taken literally, but is applied to only 11 fifths, it would amount to a rough meantone. It would be sensible to examine the results of the instructions using regular tempering values between 1/4 syntonic comma (which would yield some pure major thirds) to 1/12 Pythagorean comma (which would yield equally tempered thirds), and to deviate from the regular tempering amount on the fifths marked in the manuscript.

The first sequence

The first sequence involves tuning all twelve fifths in the cycle, which means there is no 'wolf'. The instruction to 'bear up a little' at the mark, probably means to raise the pitch a little from its otherwise tempered position, so the fifths A-E and C sharp – G sharp are to be wider than they would otherwise be, and B flat -F will be narrower.

(The mark on the manuscript is no more than a vertical dash of about the same height as the semibreves, and its identification with one particular note of each pair does seem to be quite clear).

The instruction at bar 17 is ambiguous, because it seems to require re-tuning the G sharp (just tuned as an octave from the preceding A flat) from a C sharp that has not yet been tuned. The widening of this fifth could only sensibly be achieved by flattening the C sharp.

Although the mark is associated with the G sharp, one could argue it is the C sharp that is to be raised, which would narrow the fifth more. The same point in the second sequence, however, clearly indicates the G sharp is to be raised.

The second sequence

The second sequence follows a pattern identifiable with that used in meantone tuning. The fifths circulate 'clockwise' from C as far as G sharp, and 'anticlockwise' from C as far as E flat, leaving the interval G sharp – E flat untuned.

G sharp- E flat is one of the usual positions to have the 'wolf' in meantone tuning, and in the tuning under examination here, would be the most tempered fifth, or a 'wolf', depending on the amount of tempering in the regular fifths.

There are more possible practical interpretations of this sequence because the untuned interval G sharp – E flat can be tempered by any amount required, in order to maintain a total tempering round the circle of 'fifths' of 24 cents.

General interpretation

The general idea given by the instructions can be represented on the Circle, Fig 10:

Fig 10

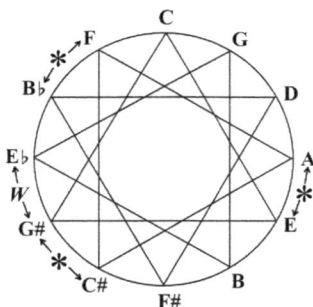

Here, the asterisks mark the intervals where we are told to 'bear a little upward', and the W marks the potential 'wolf' interval in the second sequence. This latter does not have to be a 'wolf', but in the second sequence it is not actually tuned, so it will absorb and contain any difference between a Pythagorean comma and the total accumulative tempering in the other eleven intervals.

Given the ambiguity in the manuscript, there are various interpretations one could make considering tuning on the harpsichord alone. We do not know the origin of the manuscript, or even if the ambiguities arise simply from the fact that its author's own understanding of the tempering principles was questionable (assuming the author was not Abel himself).

Let us for a moment postulate that for the reasons stated above, the intended temperament 'had the viol in mind', in order to make a better match between keyboard and viol, and accommodate the viol's own tuning parameters. Then the possibilities are more limited. Rather than converting the Circle to a data vector and making an impartial analysis, some good old fashioned lateral thinking is called for, using the Circle itself, and knowledge of the viol's characteristics.

Our premiss is that major thirds (whose quality is no small issue in early music, especially amongst good viol players) sound nicer when they are 'sweeter', or less widely tempered (in Equal Temperament they are a considerable 2/3 comma wider than 'pure' – about 1/6 semitone).

This is not merely a limited personal preference, but is consistent with the predominant trend in unequal early temperaments, both regular and irregular, to have the 'sweetest' thirds in the 'home' keys and the most grossly tempered ones in the 'remote' keys.

Looking at the straight lines 'defining' the major thirds, and the positions of the 'altered intervals', gives some clues. The viol, we remember, has open strings tuned in fourths, with a major third between the middle two strings C – E. The strings are D(1st), A(2nd), E(3rd), C(4th), G(5th), D(6th), A(7th). We also remember that when an interval is tempered narrow, its inversion will be tempered wide, and *vice versa*.

Narrowing A – E as indicated on the Circle would be entirely sensible. This would result in a widened fourth E(3rd) – A(2nd). Tuning the viol, widening of one more of the adjacent open string intervals is essential if the 1st and 6th open strings are to form a double octave.

We would expect at least one open string fourth to be wide, and sensibly more, so that the whole comma does not have to be put between one pair of strings. Similarly, the third C(4th) – E(3rd) is usually set wide to some degree.

In the Circle, the more tempering narrow we have on the arc across a major third's straight line, the 'sweeter' the third. Assuming all the unmarked fifths are either pure or equally narrow, this extra narrowing of A – E will ensure major chords in the 'home' keys of C, G , D and A, will all be equally 'sweet'.

We would not now expect further 'remote' keys to be more 'sweet' than these 'home' keys. Assuming the three asterisked intervals to be tempered the same, then the tempering in C sharp – G sharp would add the key of E to our list of equally 'sweet' home keys.

So far so good. But unless the 'W' interval G sharp – E flat is *wide*, the next four 'remote' keys B, F sharp, C sharp and G sharp, will all be 'sweeter' than our 'home' keys. So let us assume the simplest scenario, that the 'W' interval G sharp – E flat is indeed wide by the same amount that the asterisked intervals are each narrow. Then what happens is that all the thirds are equally as 'sweet' except G sharp (now nominally A flat) to C, and F to A. The F to A is one interval we would still want to be 'sweet'.

However, the usual situation on the viol is that if one wants to aim for both a 'sweet' F(1st fret, 3rd string) to A(open 2nd), and a good C(open 4th) to F, especially for sustained chords, then a single fret position will not do for both. One already expects to 'play over the fret' for an F – A, which is all that would be necessary in the case of this temperament.

Mathematically, there is only one set of tempering values that fits the above scenario, assuming the unmarked fifths round the Circle are left untempered. This is shown in Fig 11.

Fig 11

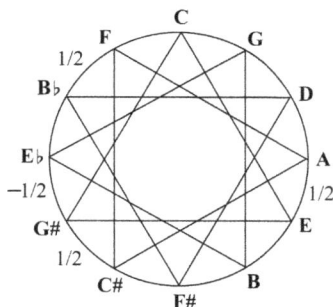

The three tempered intervals are narrowed by ½ comma, whilst the G sharp – E flat is wide by ½ comma. The 'sweet' thirds will be wide by ½ comma, which is somewhat better than Equal Temperament in which they would be 2/3 comma wide.

Fig 12 shows this temperament translated into fret positions, aligned by the second fret, as before. The result is no more conclusive than that for Equal Temperament, but equally 'possible', except again, for that excessively large space between the first and second frets on the painted viol, which is still not really explained.

Fig 12

Temperament, Fig 11

Abel

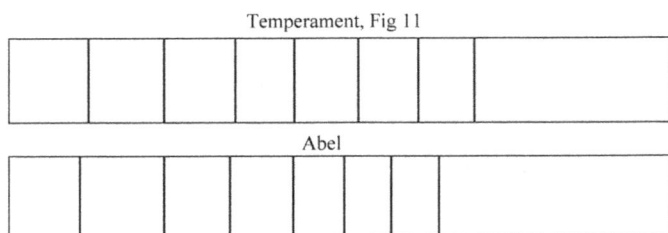

An unsuspected result

The other possible permutations for the meaning of the phrase 'bear a little upwards' at each of the three positions, involve having these intervals consecutively wide, wide, narrow, or narrow, narrow, wide, etc., compared to various 'background states' in the unmarked intervals, from 'pure' (untempered) to tempered narrow by a full ¼ comma.

None of the permutations yield any more interesting result with respect to the fret positions in Gainsborough's painting - except one, that is, if we position the first fret to satisfy the correct semitone for the E to F on the 3rd string or A to B flat on the 2nd string (rather than the C to C sharp on the C string).

As we have said, one often does this in any case, even in 'quasi-equal temperament' tuning of the viol. Then the first three frets, which are in practice the most critical in adapting the viol to a given temperament, show a remarkable correlation.

This one 'interpretation' (ironically) comes from taking the instructions in the manuscript literally, which results in 8 pure fifths, 2 wide by 'a little', one narrow by 'a little', and one 'wolf'.

am not suggesting this correlation means this is what Abel intended – such a tuning I have already stated is not really sensible or practical, and the notion that there is any connection between the manuscript instructions and Gainsborough's painting is in any case at this stage only hypothesis. The correlation is shown in Fig 13.

Fig 13

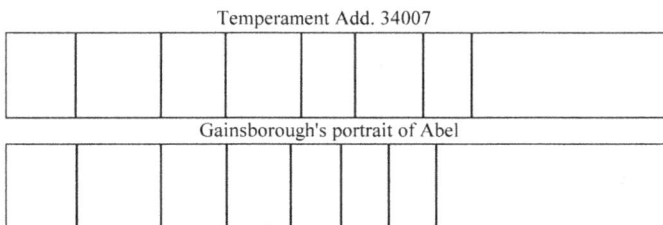

Temperament Add. 34007

Gainsborough's portrait of Abel

Given that the 'lower' fret spacing is very unusual, then compared to the large number of other contenders that do not match, this correlation is indeed remarkable.

Changing the interpretation of 'a little' in the phrase 'bear a little upward' from 2 cents (Equal Temperament type tempering) to 4 cents (roughly a 1/6 comma meantone amount, for example) makes very little difference visually.

It is worth reiterating that on the painting, it is the first three frets that are most accurately and 'deliberately' depicted with regard to minor detail, when viewed at close quarters. The higher (further from the nut) frets on a viol are typically moved to provide suitable tuning results for various intervals between stopped notes on different strings, rather than reflecting the semitone sequence on the C string.

This is common practice for equal or unequal temperament, but the number of possibilities are large. On the viol, most playing takes place in the region of the first few frets, often using open strings.

It still remains that the overall amount to which the painted higher frets extend down the fingerboard, is not as great as we would expect in order to depict the temperament in the manuscript.

The height of the instrument's action, and strings 'stopping sharp' might account for some of this, as might the same 'artistic' considerations that we proposed in relation to Equal Temperament. Also, it is possible that these frets were drawn or painted after, or before the first three, at another sitting, possibly even without the viol, or with a different viol.

A preliminary drawing for the painting also exists in the National Portrait Galley,[41] with the viol being held in a much higher position. The viol in the drawing looks like a different, larger viol, judging by the shape of the scroll, the 'f

' holes, and the position of the bridge in relation to these. (The setting to Abel's right is also different. The drawing shows a window with a high sill, but the painting shows what could be a full height shutter, with a lower surface behind Abel's right hand, on which there is a quill and a cylindrical box).

The lengths of the fingerboards on the two viols differ by roughly 6.5 %, which could be about a 3 cm difference on a viol that size. No frets appear in the drawing.

We are therefore left with this final question: Is this mysterious, apparent correlation between the instructions in Lbl Add. 34007 and Gainsborough's portrait, mere coincidence, or does it suggest something more interesting about Gainsborough's portrait of Abel, and its context?

References

[1] NPG 5947, c. 1765

[2] Dated 1777.

[3] Information kindly supplied by the Registrar of the National Portrait Gallery. The provenance of the painting has been:

1.   Mr Briggs
2.   Mr Compton
3.   Dr Hoskins, c. 1856
4.   Dr WH Cummings, FSA, acquired c. 1870; Sold Christie's, 12th December 1915 (Lot 145, bought by Sulley)
5.   Carl P Dannet, New York, by 1923
6.   National Portrait Gallery, 1987

[4]Cudworth, C, 'Gainsborough and Music', *Gainsborough, English Music, and the Fitzwilliam*, Cambridge, 1977;
Cyr, M, 'Carl Friederich Abel's Solos – a musical offering to Gainsborough?', *MT* No.1732, Vol 128, June 1987;
Wilson, MI, 'Gainsborough Bath and Music', *Apollo* Vol CV, Feb 1977;
Fulcher, GW, *The Life of Thomas Gainsborough*, London, 1856, pp 54-6;
Woodall, M, *The Letters of Thomas Gainsborough*, London, 1961, letter to David Garrick, No.31, p 71

[5] Angelo, *op. cit.*, and Jackson, William (of Exeter), *Thirty Letters on Various Subjects*, London, 1782.

[6] Angelo, Vol 1, p 184-186; ed. Lord De Walden, Howard, New York and London, 1969, pp 142-3.

[7] Angelo, H, *Reminiscences*, Vol 1, London, 1830-33, 184-187 (Benjamin Blom edition, 1969, p 141). Angelo (ed Lord De Walden, *op. cit.*, p 144) also draws attention to the inaccuracy of William Jackson's story ridiculing Gainsborough's musical abilities, found in Jackson, William (of Exeter), 'Character of Gainsborough', *The Four Ages; together with Essays on Various Subjects*, London, 1798.

Jackson's ridicule of Gainsborough could have been prompted by an uncomfortable awareness of their relative professional success.

[8] Wilson, *op. cit*;
Thicknesse, Philip, *A Sketch of the Life and Paintings of Thomas Gainsborough Esq.*, London, 1788.

[9] Parke, WT, *Musical Memoirs*, New York, 1970, p 14 (Original, London, 1830). The Rev. Bate was a pupil of Newby, the principal 'cellist of the Theatre Royal, Drury Lane.

[10] Whitley, WT, *Thomas Gainsborough*, London, 1915, p 362.

[11] Three Jayes and two Barak Normans. Woodall, *op. cit.*, Letter to William Jackson, No 56, p 115.

[12] Jackson, William, 'Character of Gainsborough', *The Four Ages*, *op. cit.*, p 160.

[13] Obtained with kind permission of the Registrar of the National Portrait Gallery.

[14] Gafurio, Franchino, *Practica musicae*, Milan, 1496; Noted by Riemann, Hugo, *Geschichte der Musiktheorie*, Berlin, 1898, p 327; Cited in Murray Barbour, J, *Tuning and Temperament*, New York, 1972, p 25.

[15] The Pythagoreans were steeped in secrecy, and there are no extant writings by Pythagoras himself.

[16] The most notable amongst the 'ancients' being Aristotle.

[17] Ptolemy's system (late 1st or early 2nd century AD) was, however, heavily indebted to Hipparchus (BC c.190-c.120).

[18] Taub, LC, *Ptolemy's universe*, Chicago & LaSalle, Illinois, 1993, pp. 125-127; Barker, A, *Greek musical writings*, Vol. 2, Cambridge, 1989, pp 278, 375-376. On the *kanon*, see pp 291; 319; 340-345; 362 ff.

[19] *Harmonics*, Book III, Chapters 4, 8-16; Barker, A, *Greek musical writings*, (2 Vols), Cambridge, 1989, Vol. 2, pp. 375-376; 380-391;

Solomon, J, *Harmony in Ptolemy's Harmonics*, Armidale, NSW, 1990, pp 15-16.

[20] Solomon, J, *ibid.*, p. 13.

[21] It is somewhat more compromised in the case of the clavichord, and we here are excluding electronic instruments.

[22] In other words, if an instrument's acoustical tone structures are built on harmonic principles, involving the Pythagorean ratios, then temperament theory will 'fit' the instrument perfectly.

[23] The theory does, however, result in the appearance of 'irrational fractions' that cannot be expressed with perfect precision.

[24] Using the Equally Tempered semitone as a datum.

[25] The principles of the 'tuning meter' are often misunderstood. All tuning meters incorporate an 'error tolerance', without which they would actually be impractical or impossible to use.

The meter has to match the physical accuracy with which the instrument can be tuned, and the physical skill with which the average person can tune it. If the meter's 'sensitivity' exceeded this, it would be impractical for the task.

When a meter indicates a note is 'correct', it does not mean 'perfectly correct according to the mathematical definition of the temperament', or even 'correct according to the judgement of an expert tuner'. It actually means 'the note is now within the range that the meter will accept as correct'.

For example, by the standards of practical temperament definition that are applicable to a concert piano, which is a very high precision, extremely high tension instrument, inexpensive tuning meters are very, very crude indeed.

The most expensive piano tuning meters, which themselves can cost as much as a piano, still do not match the physical accuracy with which the piano *can* be tuned, or the physical skill with which the artist tuner can tune it.

This may seem strange, until one realises that accuracy of tuning is in practice not so much about achieving a set of prescribed note frequencies, as about setting relationships of the acoustical spectra belonging to the various notes.

[26] It also does not obey the straightforward laws that it does on, for example, piano or harpsichord strings.

[27] One reason is: A major feature of the quality of an interval that a given temperament determines, is its beat rate. The beat rate is also an objective 'index' of the interval's true size. Intervals tuned on the viol by matching note for note unisons with the same notes on the harpsichord, will often have different beat rates to the harpsichord.

This is a feature of matching the tuning of viols and harpsichords, that has nothing to do with the dichotomy in the required positions of frets in unequal temperaments. The set of beat rates in an unequal keyboard temperament, is not accurately reproduced as the same set, when applying the temperament to the viol.

[28] The cent is 1/100 of an equally tempered semitone, or 1/1200 of a perfect octave.

[29] It is also possible to represent the intervals and their relationships as geometric ratios. The use of geometry prior to decimal notation (first quarter of 17th century, Stevinus and Napier) also had the advantage that it could in effect express irrational numbers, which is why some (but by no means all) Greeks regarded it as a science superior to arithmetic.

[30] Meantone, by the contemporary definition. There are reasons why some scholars argue ¼ comma meantone is the only true meantone.

[31] Aron, Pietro, *Toscanello in musica*, Venice, 1523; 1529.

[32] In common parlance 'generality' usually implies vagueness, but in science and mathematics general laws and formulae are the 'highest form' from which specific instances can be shown to be derived.

[33] Capleton, B, *Carl Friedrich Abel and the Viola da Gamba: A Study of Lbl Add. 31697 and its Context*, Appendix C, MMusRCM dissertation, Royal College of Music, 1994.

[34] The computations and graph data generation were executed in Mathcad.

[35] Helm, SM, *Carl Frederich Abel, symphonist: a biographical, stylistic and bibliographical study*, Michigan, 1953, p 100.

[36] MS NYPL, Drexel 5871.

[37] Lbl Add. 31697.

[38] The second piece is not an Abel composition, but an arrangement (without bass) of the melody in G, 'Qui sdegno' from Mozart's *Il Flauto Magico*.

[39] Mortimer's *London Universal Directory*, 1763, Library of the Guildhall, London. See 'An eighteenth-century directory of London Musicians', *GSJ*, II, pp 27-31.

[40] In reality, it would produce a scale in which tempering in the different keys could be better described as 'roughly the same, but with random differences'.

[41] No. 5081

www.ingramcontent.com/pod-product-compliance
Lightning Source LLC
Chambersburg PA
CBHW060538030426
42337CB00021B/4335